AF439385

DAILY MESSAGES FROM MOTHER MALIA: THE GREAT MOTHER

Best-Selling Author and Founder of
International #1 Akashic Records Training School

Jennifer Longmore

DAILY MESSAGES FROM MOTHER MALIA: THE GREAT MOTHER

Best-Selling Author and Founder of
International #1 Akashic Records Training School

Jennifer Longmore

First paperback edition - March 2024

Paperback ISBN: 979-8-8692-6992-8

PRINTED IN THE UNITED STATES OF AMERICA ON ACID-FREE PAPER

Published by E.P. House
www.ephouse.co

Table of Contents

Daily Reflections

In the stillness, we find ourselves seeking solace. In these moments of quiet we often yearn for guidance—a beacon of light to illuminate our path.

This book, your companion for the next 365 days, is a vessel that carries the wisdom and compassion of Mother Malia, your spiritual guide who imparts her knowledge with the gentle, nurturing love of a great mother.

Each day, Mother Malia will share a message with you, a whisper of wisdom to carry in your heart as you navigate the day. These messages are meant to inspire and suggest. They are candles to light your path. Each message is a gift; a seed of thought for you to nurture throughout your day.

After reading each message, take a moment to close your eyes. Imagine how the day's message can support you in that moment. Visualize it as a force—a pulsating orb of light within you. Feel its warmth, its power, and allow it to permeate your being. This is your moment of connection, your bridge between the spiritual and the physical—the ethereal and the earthly. Use the space after Mother Malia's message to visualize and journal about how it can support you in that very moment.

Then, at the day's end, Mother Malia invites you to return, reflect and journal again about your day and the journey you have undertaken with her message. This reflection is a moment of reconciliation, a chance to restore balance and harmony within you. It is the sacred silence where you listen to the echoes of your day, the resonating frequencies of your experiences, and how they have been touched by the wisdom of Mother Malia.

This book is not merely a collection of daily spiritual guides. With Mother Malia's wisdom as your compass, each sunrise will greet you with the promise of a new beginning, and each sunrise cradle you in her arms of warmth and peace.

Just as bees are drawn to the sweetness of honey, so, too, was your life destined to be filled with divine perfection.

Note from the Author

Please enjoy your daily ascension messages designed to
restore your original codes in divine perfection.

You are the blessing, the ceremony, and the celebration.
You are the answer and the solution.

You are the anointing of divine perfection.

Golden blessings,
Mother Malia: The Great Mother

JANUARY
New Beginnings

January 1

Welcome to a new canvas to create your beautiful year and blissful life. I invite you to commune with your body to ask it how it would like to be celebrated, adorned, anointed into this bountiful new year!

Visualize:

....

....

....

....

....

....

....

....

Reflect:

....

....

....

....

....

....

....

January 2

Now that you have communed with your body, I invite you to commune with your home—that houses your body, that houses your divinity. How does your home wish to be adorned, celebrated, anointed to the blessings of this new year? What would you like to be removed from its temple, and how does it wish to hold you in your divine mission this year?

Visualize:

Reflect:

January 3

Beloved one, your energy is infinite when you choose divine perfection. If you are not feeling energized, this is your invitation to return from such emotions as worry, judgment, guilt, shame or other denser energies. There is only lightness when returning to divine perfection.

Visualize:

Reflect:

January 4

Your annoyances are your anointings. What is annoying you right now, and what is the invitation to step into?

Visualize:

Reflect:

January 5

Collapsing time is a distortion. It creates the illusion of needing to rush because time is running out. It creates impatience. That is not of divine perfection.

Visualize:

....

....

....

....

....

....

....

....

Reflect:

....

....

....

....

....

....

....

....

January 6

The Bee is the timekeeper. She knows how to expand time—this is divine perfection. In this space, it can feel like several days are rolled into one. So, would you prefer to enjoy this glorious day or would you prefer to collapse time and "get things over with?" Which one feels light, easy and joyful?

Visualize:

Reflect:

January 7

Each moment is a sacred new beginning. Enjoy the wonder
of this today.

Visualize:

....

....

....

....

....

....

....

Reflect:

....

....

....

....

....

....

....

January 8

Spreading laughter is a divine contribution. Just like the dolphins and the whales, when they spread their voice, it amplifies the resonance on the earth plane and supports restoration of divine perfection instantly.

Visualize:

Reflect:

January 9

There is no judgment in divine perfection. Only love, beauty, joy, peace and abundance.

Visualize:

....
....
....
....
....
....
....
....

Reflect:

....
....
....
....
....
....
....
....

January 10

What if the roadblocks are presenting you the invitation to journey down a different path? What if that is divine perfection blessing you by moving you towards what is already meant for you?

Visualize:

Reflect:

January 11

If you are wondering why you are unclear in your awareness, instead ask "why would I expect it to be there if I am always giving it away and deciding that it is not there?" Awareness is always present, using it in service to our sacred path is the way in and the way through.

Visualize:

....
....
....
....
....
....
....
....

Reflect:

....
....
....
....
....
....
....
....

January 12

If you desire a new world, it requires a new perception, a new way of contributing, a new way of understanding your sacred part of it all. The Land of the People need your sacred elixir and are delighted to receive it and be blessed by it.

Visualize:

Reflect:

January 13

Spiritual insignificance serves no one. Deciding that you matter, and you always have, will allow you to serve fully.

Visualize:

....
....
....
....
....
....
....
....

Reflect:

....
....
....
....
....
....
....
....

January 14

Where are you hooked into nostalgia and how might it be holding you back
from claiming all that is already waiting to bless you?

Visualize:

Reflect:

January 15

Being here now is the greatest lesson and the greatest gift.

Visualize:

Reflect:

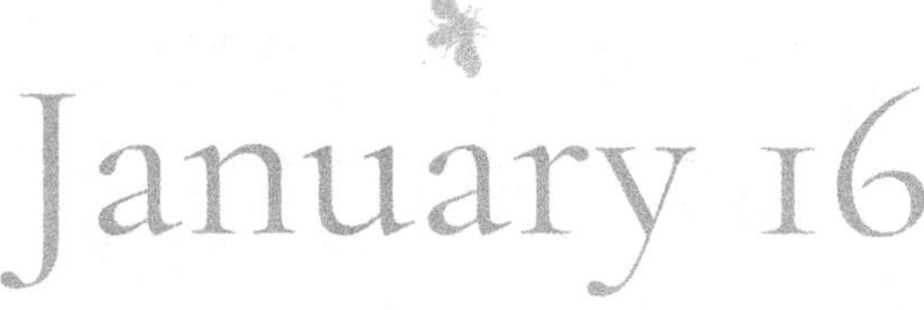

January 16

If you are attached to objects and money over honoring you, divine perfection
will evade you.

Visualize:

....
....
....
....
....
....
....
....

Reflect:

....
....
....
....
....
....
....
....

January 17

You are the ceremony. You are the celebration. You are divine.

Visualize:

Reflect:

January 18

The beautiful thing about endings is that they are also entry points to new beginnings.

Visualize:

Reflect:

January 19

There is no need to dwell on "what if." What if it doesn't work out? What if I fail? Release yourself from that mental torture. The mind creates problems, the heart creates rhythm for your life.

Visualize:

....
....
....
....
....
....
....
....

Reflect:

....
....
....
....
....
....
....
....

January 20

You're never "too old," "too young," or "too late" to do anything. You are infinite and capable of creating anew in any moment.

Visualize:

Reflect:

January 21

You are wired to use your vision and share it far and wide. If you do not choose how you use it, it will be chosen for you. Your natural desire to place your eyes, your vision on something could pull you into the perpetual vortex of the screens, or the artificial agenda if you are not choosing how to honor the sacredness of your sight.

Visualize:

Reflect:

January 22

There is no need for answers when you *are* the answer.

Visualize:

Reflect:

January 23

When you are fearing a new beginning, ask yourself, "What will this mean for me? What would my life look like in this newness?" More often than not, knowing the answer is all you need to realize if it's worth it to choose.

Visualize:

Reflect:

January 24

Never fear rejection. In divine perfection, nothing is personal.

Visualize:

Reflect:

January 25

If you are waiting to feel ready, you have stepped out of divine perfection. It brings things to you, so there is no need to prepare when you are ready to receive.

Visualize:

....

....

....

....

....

....

....

....

Reflect:

....

....

....

....

....

....

....

January 26

What a blessing to clear out your closet, your home and your mind. What new
and aligned energies have you created space for now?

Visualize:

Reflect:

January 27

Pay attention to the little miracles today, there are bigger ones on the way once you attune your signals to looking for miracles in every moment.

Visualize:

....
....
....
....
....
....
....
....

Reflect:

....
....
....
....
....
....
....

January 28

You have already have the deep knowing to move on when it's time. Allow divine perfection to clear the way for you.

Visualize:

Reflect:

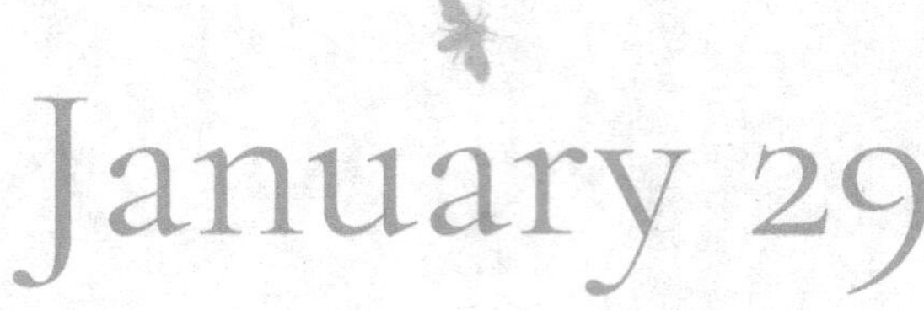

January 29

You are limitless. Allowing limits to move you through the world extracts you
from divine perfection where there is only bliss and effortless flow.

Visualize:

....

....

....

....

....

....

....

....

Reflect:

....

....

....

....

....

....

....

....

January 30

Starting over keeps you on the hamster wheel, as it never ends. What if you are simply making space for new choices and new energies?

Visualize:

Reflect:

January 31

Your life gets to be as colorful, joyful and blissful as you desire.

Visualize:

....
....
....
....
....
....
....
....

Reflect:

....
....
....
....
....
....
....
....

FEBRUARY

Love

February 1

You are loved. You matter. You are unique. Your presence on this planet is honored.

Visualize:

....

....

....

....

....

....

....

....

Reflect:

....

....

....

....

....

....

....

....

February 2

It costs nothing to spread love. It is everything to *be* love.

Visualize:

Reflect:

February 3

Your heart is a blessing to the collective heartbeat.

Visualize:

....
....
....
....
....
....
....
....

Reflect:

....
....
....
....
....
....
....
....

February 4

Allow divine perfection to calibrate all relationships to be a blessing to you.

Visualize:

Reflect:

February 5

Allow divine perfection to call awake a sacred union for you.

Visualize:

....
....
....
....
....
....
....
....

Reflect:

....
....
....
....
....
....
....

February 6

You are not a project to be fixed. You do not need to do anything to be more lovable. You are divine perfection.

Visualize:

Reflect:

February 7

Most people have one foot in and one foot out in relationships, whether its a friend, lover or family member. They're either looking and waiting for a reason to walk away or looking for a way to jump in with both feet. It's really not about you, so please don't make yourself wrong for the push and pull that many create. It's okay for you to require emotional maturity from others which involves open communication, personal responsibility and respect in order to remain eligible to remain in *your* energy field.

Visualize:

....

....

....

....

....

....

....

....

Reflect:

....

....

....

....

....

....

....

....

February 8

Your voice has a harmonic resonance that is received as a sacred melody for the heart. Please share it often.

Visualize:

Reflect:

February 9

If you knew divine perfection was always working in your favor, would you be able to step out of perpetual questioning and into full living?

Visualize:

....
....
....
....
....
....
....
....

Reflect:

....
....
....
....
....
....
....
....

February 10

Divine perfection transmutes sexual trauma so that you can experience sacred intimacy.

Visualize:

....

....

....

....

....

....

....

....

Reflect:

....

....

....

....

....

....

....

....

February 11

There is no need to heal in divine perfection. It is the ultimate restorer of radiant health. Simply choose it and witness the miracles that pour into your life.

Visualize:

Reflect:

February 12

Love is in the air. It is also in the land, in the water, in your heart, and all
around. You are always surrounded by its presence.

Visualize:

Reflect:

February 13

Your attention creates the reality that you are now experiencing. If your attention is focused on anything other than love, you now know what to shift into to create a different experience.

Visualize:

....

....

....

....

....

....

....

Reflect:

....

....

....

....

....

....

....

February 14

Judgment keeps love at bay.

Visualize:

Reflect:

February 15

Not everyone can receive love, as it has been tainted for them. Perhaps they were taught that love is violent and if people fight with each other they are fighting "for" each other. Perhaps they learned that love is abusive. "I only hit you because I love you!" When people cannot receive it, it does not mean to stop spreading it. The people who can't are the ones who require a bigger dose.

Visualize:

Reflect:

February 16

The greatest blessing to all, including you, is love.

Visualize:

Reflect:

February 17

Ego is the enemy of partnership. When solving a conflict becomes confused
with a need to "win" or "be right" a barrier is built upon that partnership. When
you break it down, true partnership can begin.

Visualize:

Reflect:

February 18

We have a great, unlimited resource that resides right within us. It is our capacity to love and our abundance is limitless when we recognize this.

Visualize:

Reflect:

February 19

There will be people who will try to pull you into their storm. Don't let yourself
get dragged into it. Instead, love them through the tumult and pull them into
your calm.

Visualize:

Reflect:

February 20

Set the example for others: love yourself so well that they never question how to love you.

Visualize:

Reflect:

February 21

You cannot wait to begin loving yourself until you are 100 percent satisfied with who you are. If you wait until you have "fixed" yourself, you will never be satisfied. Your journey to self-love cannot wait until you decide you are worthy. It is needed even more when you do not feel worthy.

Visualize:

Reflect:

February 22

When you are attuned to divine perfection, your frequency becomes love.

Visualize:

Reflect:

February 23

Love does not find you. It *is* you.

Visualize:

Reflect:

February 24

Chasing love is unnecessary once you trust that divine perfection is always
working in your favor and bringing it to you instead.

Visualize:

Reflect:

February 25

Love cannot be lost. It may take a different form, but it is not lost.

Visualize:

....
....
....
....
....
....
....
....

Reflect:

....
....
....
....
....
....
....
....

February 26

The best things to invest into your relationship are time and lots of laughter.

Visualize:

Reflect:

February 27

If you fill yourself all the way up with love, it has no choice but to spill over into others.

Visualize:

Reflect:

February 28

You attract the quality of love that you think you deserve. Allow your heart to be wiser than your mind.

Visualize:

Reflect:

MARCH
New Perspectives

March 1

Most people are doing their best, even if it may not seem that way to you. In divine perfection, nothing is personal.

Visualize:

....
....
....
....
....
....
....

Reflect:

....
....
....
....
....
....
....
....

March 2

Instead of using your mind to plant new seeds of creation, choose divine perfection instead. It is always creating the most divine outcomes for you.

Visualize:

Reflect:

March 3

Return to the divine truth of who you really are, before the world told you that you were not enough.

Visualize:

Reflect:

March 4

You have the power to choose. You can choose from *fear* or from *faith*. You can choose in contraction or in expansion. You can choose in anger or in love. You have the power to *choose*.

Visualize:

Reflect:

March 5

Worrying doesn't tackle tomorrow's problems, but it does interfere with today's peace.

Visualize:

Reflect:

March 6

You always have a choice. Every choice has a cause and effect. Choose your perceptions, flow state and actions with divine intention.

Visualize:

Reflect:

March 7

Instead of being on the verge of a breakdown, what if you were on the precipice of a miraculous breakthrough?

Visualize:

Reflect:

March 8

You are not broken and in need of fixing. You are hurt and in need of love.

Visualize:

Reflect:

March 9

You already belong, you are a blessing and your sacred elixir is needed.

Visualize:

....
....
....
....
....
....
....
....

Reflect:

....
....
....
....
....
....
....

March 10

Momentum is already inherent in divine flow. Resistance to natural rhythms and ways of being is what creates the perception of being stuck or stagnant.

Visualize:

Reflect:

March 11

Timelines can be expanded to allow you to bask in even more miracles and bounty in your life. Think in terms of expansion instead of time.

Visualize:

....
....
....
....
....
....
....
....

Reflect:

....
....
....
....
....
....
....
....

March 12

The grass isn't greener on the other side. It's greener where you see blades of emerald light instead of a nuisance that needs to be weeded.

Visualize:

Reflect:

March 13

Motivation is unnecessary when you allow divine perfection to bring to you
what you desire. Motivation is not required when dancing with what lights you
up.

Visualize:

....

....

....

....

....

....

....

....

Reflect:

....

....

....

....

....

....

....

....

March 14

Change is inevitable. It's your relationship with it that determines your experience.

Visualize:

Reflect:

March 15

Clutter is present to the degree that you are choosing to be busy over purposeful.

Visualize:

....
....
....
....
....
....
....
....

Reflect:

....
....
....
....
....
....
....
....

March 16

Suffering is a part of this distorted reality. In divine perfection, there is only bliss.

Visualize:

Reflect:

March 17

Perhaps you were sent places to spread blessings, and isn't that divine?

Visualize:

Reflect:

March 18

When you move through crowded spaces, envision your golden light sprinkling everywhere to bless all in the space.

Visualize:

Reflect:

March 19

Thoughts and perceptions are different. The quality of your life is determined by how much time you reside in your heart.

Visualize:

Reflect:

March 20

Complications are misplaced distractions from an unconscious attachment to solving problems. In divine perfection, there are no questions or problems, only answers.

Visualize:

Reflect:

March 21

When you feel exhausted, tired and spent, teach yourself to rest, not to quit.

Visualize:

Reflect:

March 22

Being an impeccable steward of your consciousness will allow more financial
flow.

Visualize:

Reflect:

March 23

Instead of demanding that the Universe flow your way, try aligning yourself with the flow of the Universe.

Visualize:

Reflect:

March 24

There are no failures in divine perfection, there is only neutrality. Failures are filtered through the lens of judgment. Neutrality is filtered through the lens of grace.

Visualize:

Reflect:

March 25

What if you were sent to reside in your current location, because that is where the greatest volume of blessings are required to hold the light?

Visualize:

Reflect:

March 26

Loneliness is not possible in divine perfection. Instead, it creates the deepest sense of connection and belonging.

Visualize:

Reflect:

March 27

Ecstasy is the highest vibration on the planet, born from a sustained state of joy. Ecstasy is the strongest magnet for all that you desire. If you desire effortless and instant manifestation, master your capacity to hold sustained joy.

Visualize:

Reflect:

March 28

Instead of doing your best, shift into being the fullest expression of your light.
One places pressure, the other creates expansion.

Visualize:

Reflect:

March 29

Choosing divine perfection creates instant and boundless vitality and radiance.

Visualize:

Reflect:

March 30

Everything you desire to know is on the other side of choosing to sustain your capacity to be in awareness.

Visualize:

Reflect:

March 31

Stewardship of your channel of consciousness determines your capacity to fully
& clearly channel consciousness.

Visualize:

....

....

....

....

....

....

....

....

Reflect:

....

....

....

....

....

....

....

....

APRIL

The Things That Help the Soul Blossom

April 1

The opinions and projections of others don't impact when you reside in divine perfection, because everything is neutral.

Visualize:

....
....
....
....
....
....
....
....

Reflect:

....
....
....
....
....
....
....

April 2

Looking outside of yourself for answers is always going to feel off since you are the answer, and the answers already reside within.

Visualize:

....
....
....
....
....
....
....
....

Reflect:

....
....
....
....
....
....
....
....

April 3

When you feel off, and you don't feel like you can access your own awareness, the best antidote to this is nature. The harmony of elixirs available to you will transport you back to divine perfection.

Visualize:

Reflect:

April 4

Emotions are not good or bad, they are simply information for how much you are "doing" versus "being."

Visualize:

Reflect:

April 5

The truth may sting but the pain is temporary. Illusion may feel comforting yet causes for more lasting suffering.

Visualize:

....
....
....
....
....
....
....
....

Reflect:

....
....
....
....
....
....
....
....

April 6

The artificial agenda wants your most precious resource: your consciousness.
Divine perfection only has one agenda, and that is to restore original
consciousness so that you may thrive on the Land of the People. One controls,
the other honors your field of sovereignty.

Visualize:

Reflect:

April 7

Love-bombing and ghosting are both products of unhealthy attachment to the sacred feminine. Divine perfection is the way through since it is the deepest connection to the divine mother.

Visualize:

Reflect:

April 8

When people claim to know it all they are secretly fearing that they don't know much and will be found out. They choose to posture or even copy other people's knowledge and pass it off as their own to protect their deep secret that they do not know enough, which really translates to them not feeling enough all around. We can judge or punish them, but in divine perfection there is only neutrality and the desire for them to choose more for themselves, if they are willing.

Visualize:

Reflect:

April 9

You are not only the priority, you are the blessing and the celebration.

Visualize:

::

::

::

::

::

::

::

::

Reflect:

::

::

::

::

::

::

::

::

April 10

You are allowed to give yourself space from people that are committed to suffering.

Visualize:

Reflect:

April 11

You are allowed to hold sacred boundaries for those who try to pull you into
toxic triangles to serve their own agendas.

Visualize:

....
....
....
....
....
....
....
....

Reflect:

....
....
....
....
....
....
....
....

April 12

Misidentified expectations usually lead to misery and disappointment. Choosing divine perfection will allow you to bask in constant delight.

Visualize:

Reflect:

April 13

Divine perfection allows you to truly see yourself as divine. Flaws you once saw disappear. You see yourself in beauty and that liberates you to spread your sacred elixir with joy.

Visualize:

....
....
....
....
....
....
....
....

Reflect:

....
....
....
....
....
....
....
....

April 14

Meditating is an easy way to anoint yourself with more blessings and divine coding.

Visualize:

....
....
....
....
....
....
....
....

Reflect:

....
....
....
....
....
....
....
....

April 15

Worthiness is something that is so deeply understood in divine perfection that it no longer needs to be a part of the conversation.

Visualize:

Reflect:

April 16

Inspiration is the product of your vision deciding to play in a bigger playground.

Visualize:

Reflect:

April 17

You may feel like you're losing your mind when you become a clear channel of consciousness, which won't be the case. However, if you were to lose something on your channeling journey, the mind isn't the worst thing you could lose.

Visualize:

Reflect:

April 18

There is no balance, as that is an illusion. Harmony is what you actually desire.

Visualize:

....

....

....

....

....

....

....

....

Reflect:

....

....

....

....

....

....

....

....

April 19

Looking inward shrinks your world. Why not marvel at the beauty, and the experiences that you desire to create, and hold those memories inside instead?

Visualize:

Reflect:

April 20

You are always aligned. The better question is, "what am I aligning to and is my life experience a reflection of that decision?"

Visualize:

....
....
....
....
....
....
....
....

Reflect:

....
....
....
....
....
....
....
....

April 21

The present moment is filled with presents that nurture your being.

Visualize:

Reflect:

April 22

You are a crucial part of the divine plan and your sacred elixir is needed here now. Your sacred mission is calling, are you ready to accept the call and express it to the fullest?

Visualize:

Reflect:

April 23

If hard work were the answer to creating more money, more people would be basking in financial overflow. Efforting is not required to receive, and divine perfection is here to teach you this.

Visualize:

....

....

....

....

....

....

....

....

Reflect:

....

....

....

....

....

....

....

....

April 24

You trust others' guidance to the degree that you do not trust your own. If you don't trust your own, then are you really serving your sacred path by outsourcing it to others?

Visualize:

Reflect:

April 25

Wholeness can be instantly achieved & sustained by choosing to operate fully in divine perfection.

Visualize:

Reflect:

April 26

Your time on the earth plane is both limited and infinite. Mastering time to expand at your will creates more joy, more abundance, more flow.

Visualize:

Reflect:

April 27

There is no ego in divine perfection, only love, truth and neutrality.

Visualize:

....
....
....
....
....
....
....
....

Reflect:

....
....
....
....
....
....
....
....

April 28

Consciousness is your most treasured currency. How are you stewarding it?

Visualize:

Reflect:

April 29

Falling from grace is impossible in divine perfection. It is our best teacher for mastering the art of grace.

Visualize:

Reflect:

April 30

Your purpose, in part, is to create simply ... because you can. No permission or explanation required.

Visualize:

Reflect:

MAY

Expansion & Growth

May 1

Declaring wants is very different than choosing that which you desire. Wanting is a statement, choosing is an activator and mobilizes divine perfection in your favor.

Visualize:

....
....
....
....
....
....
....
....

Reflect:

....
....
....
....
....
....
....
....

May 2

Divine perfection invites in instant clarity about what your true priorities are, and since there are only a few, it graces you with simplifying your life and creating space to truly enjoy what matters most to you. Better yet, it expands time, so that you get to savor these moments even longer than you dreamed was possible. And it is so heavenly.

Visualize:

Reflect:

May 3

Many people know their sacred path, few choose to live it fully. Those who have chosen to live it fully will tell you that they are not only fully supported, but more miraculously than they could've imagined. When you choose to perpetually bless others with no expectation of return, that is when you are blessed the most.

Visualize:

Reflect:

May 4

Underneath it all, pushing and pulling with your desires is simply you in full resistance to yourself and your sacred elixir.

Visualize:

Reflect:

May 5

The past holds nothing for you; you've already resided there. You came *here* to collect experiences to grow and cultivate wisdom that you can share, not brood in a past that will never change—no matter how long you sit on it's park bench, waiting for it to become something that it cannot be for you.

Visualize:

Reflect:

May 6

If you want to expand, widen your perspective to bask in the beauty of the entire
landscape of your sacred vision.

Visualize:

....

....

....

....

....

....

....

....

Reflect:

....

....

....

....

....

....

....

....

May 7

If you are afraid of leaving others behind, you are still attached to savior programming and the control systems that hold it in place. No one needs saving, nor do they need you to decide whether they are where they are "meant" to be. People are always choosing, even if you do not agree. Focusing on your own path will lighten the load and free you to experience more bliss.

Visualize:

Reflect:

May 8

The excuses you are judging yourself for are simply versions of you trying to get your attention, to let you know that you don't feel safe enough to take the next step on your sacred path. Everyone moves through the world at a speed that reflects how safe they feel. Divine perfection *is* divine protection. It's impossible to feel anything other than divinely supported when choosing it as your new home.

Visualize:

Reflect:

May 9

Your sacred path was never meant to look like anyone else's, so asking others for input is already a recipe for taking you off course. The mastery is in complete trust of self and divine perfection.

Visualize:

....

....

....

....

....

....

....

Reflect:

....

....

....

....

....

....

....

May 10

If you are unhappy, it's quite possible that you are living someone else's dreams for them, instead of choosing your own path with joy and delight.

Visualize:

Reflect:

May 11

Of course you can have it all, you are already infinite with access to all that you choose to claim. The issue is that you are rationing what you claim. There is so much bounty on this earth plane, you can never claim too much.

Visualize:

....
....
....
....
....
....
....
....

Reflect:

....
....
....
....
....
....
....
....

May 12

It is not someone else's job to be trustworthy to you. It's your divine responsibility to trust your awareness fully so that you can sense who has capacity to honor you—and who doesn't—and then choose your next steps with full awareness.

Visualize:

....

....

....

....

....

....

....

....

Reflect:

....

....

....

....

....

....

....

....

May 13

You are not a burden. That is a distortion. You are a blessing and you are already
blessed.

Visualize:

....

....

....

....

....

....

....

....

Reflect:

....

....

....

....

....

....

....

May 14

Are you setting boundaries or barriers? Boundaries facilitate honoring, barriers disconnect.

Visualize:

Reflect:

May 15

Crystal clarity resides in divine perfection.

Visualize:

....
....
....
....
....
....
....
....

Reflect:

....
....
....
....
....
....
....
....

May 16

There is no need to judge your past. It was always preparing you for this moment, and isn't that wonderful?

Visualize:

....
....
....
....
....
....
....
....

Reflect:

....
....
....
....
....
....
....
....

May 17

The focus in divine perfection is to bless versus heal others. The difference is palpable.

Visualize:

Reflect:

May 18

Beauty is an essential part of your sacred path. You are beauty and your sacred path is an expression of that. Imagine the trail of beautiful light codes you are spreading everywhere, and how much more beauty you are creating for others, simply by being here and moving through the world.

Visualize:

Reflect:

May 19

We are all visitors to the Land of the People. Are you going to take full advantage of your stay, or hide in your hotel room until the trip is over?

Visualize:

Reflect:

May 20

Animal medicine is more sacred than we realize. They want to bless us with it and it delights them to do so. Are you making yourself available to receive as often as you can?

Visualize:

Reflect:

May 21

Divine perfection is truth. There is no longer a need to seek or defend it in this space.

Visualize:

....
....
....
....
....
....
....
....

Reflect:

....
....
....
....
....
....
....

May 22

The desires you command arrive as quickly as the certainty you hold for their inevitably to show up and bless you.

Visualize:

Reflect:

May 23

Devotion is best channeled towards yourself as the ceremony.

Visualize:

....
....
....
....
....
....
....
....

Reflect:

....
....
....
....
....
....
....
....

May 24

There is no backwards or forwards, only flow.

Visualize:

Reflect:

May 25

Discomfort is to be celebrated, as it is the first sign you have left the comfort zone you no longer wish to reside in.

Visualize:

....
....
....
....
....
....
....
....

Reflect:

....
....
....
....
....
....
....
....

May 26

Knowing does not require evidence, only being in the truth and presence of it.

Visualize:

Reflect:

May 27

Your human experience is no more or less important than your sacred path. You are human after all, and you are here to be with others, not above them.

Visualize:

....

....

....

....

....

....

....

....

Reflect:

....

....

....

....

....

....

....

....

May 28

You are allowed to evolve, that is why we are here. Your style, your truth, your circles and your laugh are all allowed to evolve, simply because you *can*. No explanation or understanding required.

Visualize:

Reflect:

May 29

Before allowing bodyworkers to touch you, please ensure that they are approaching you from a place of wholeness. Those who view you as broken—and needing to be fixed—will often hold you in that pattern because of their need to be your savior. This is something to be cautious of. In divine perfection, there is no need for body work, as the body knows how to restore itself to its most optimum state.

Visualize:

Reflect:

May 30

What if your body, as a wise and infinite consciousness, already knows what it requires to be completely restored and invigorated?

Visualize:

Reflect:

May 31

Non-attachment creates more flow.

Visualize:

Reflect:

JUNE
Abundance

June 1

The wind does not apologize for moving leaves on trees. It is simply being wind.

Visualize:

....
....
....
....
....
....
....
....

Reflect:

....
....
....
....
....
....
....
....

June 2

Fire does not apologize for burning brightly or melting objects, it is simply being fire and doing what fire does.

Visualize:

Reflect:

June 3

Rivers do not apologize for flowing too strongly, it is simply being water and doing what water does. It also knows how to move through and around objections, instead of using them as reasons to stop the flow.

Visualize:

Reflect:

June 4

Lightning doesn't apologize for lighting up the sky and making its presence known, it is simply being light language in the sky.

Visualize:

Reflect:

June 5

The Sacred Horse is one of the most benevolent beings on the earth plane, ready to bless us with its profound ability to restore its original codes. We have a duty of care to ensure sacred stewardship of these benevolent beings.

Visualize:

Reflect:

June 6

The Sacred Cow only wants to love and nurture us, and yet it is consumed as a
two-dimensional object to satiate our gluttony and programming. Like the
Sacred Horse, they are one of the highest vibration of beings on the earth, and
yet we treat them like a commodity. If we are to restore peace and beauty to the
Land of the People, how we treat our animal elders is an essential part of this. If
we claim to desire sacred stewardship of the earth plane, it must include sacred
stewardship of the animals.

Visualize:

Reflect:

June 7

Your rooms are your wombs. They are havens of creations. How are you moving through your spaces, and what would be possible if you adopted this new awareness?

Visualize:

Reflect:

June 8

Money is simply a tool. Allow it to fully serve your sacred mission so that even more people can be blessed by your divinity.

Visualize:

Reflect:

June 9

Money is a blessing and expands as you focus on blessing others. The more you feel honored to bless others with your sacred mission, the more money arrives to support that sacred cause.

Visualize:

....
....
....
....
....
....
....
....

Reflect:

....
....
....
....
....
....
....
....

June 10

Worry is a product of moving through the world with your mind. It is impossible to access when you move through the world with your heart.

Visualize:

Reflect:

June 11

In divine perfection, there is no confusion. Crystal clear is ever present in this space.

Visualize:

....
....
....
....
....
....
....
....

Reflect:

....
....
....
....
....
....
....
....

June 12

Money is neutral in divine perfection. Your relationship to it is determined by what you project onto it. If you a view money as a blessing, it will be so.

Visualize:

Reflect:

June 13

Blame, shame and guilt are merely signs that you've stepped out of divine perfection.

Visualize:

....
....
....
....
....
....
....
....

Reflect:

....
....
....
....
....
....
....
....

June 14

The body knows how to restore itself in divine perfection. Little is needed for it to thrive when you view it as divine as opposed to broken.

Visualize:

Reflect:

June 15

Abundance is not conditional. It is everywhere. There is an abundance of beauty on earth, imagination, opportunities, flow, resources and more. When the brain is focussed on lack, accessing abundance that is already available seems out of reach when in fact it is only a slight shift in perception away.

Visualize:

....
....
....
....
....
....
....
....

Reflect:

....
....
....
....
....
....
....
....

June 16

Your capacity to receive wealth is limitless in divine perfection.

Visualize:

Reflect:

June 17

Money has its own consciousness. If you are willing to have conversations with
it, you will be amazed at how much it wishes to teach you.

Visualize:

....
....
....
....
....
....
....
....

Reflect:

....
....
....
....
....
....
....

June 18

Just like the rivers, money loves to flow simply because it can, and simply because it is in its nature to do so.

Visualize:

Reflect:

June 19

Time is easily expanded in divine perfection. It is a beautiful art to learn to master in service to your sacred mission.

Visualize:

....
....
....
....
....
....
....
....

Reflect:

....
....
....
....
....
....
....
....

June 20

Your sacred calling will continue finding new and louder ways to get your attention when you are avoiding answering the call when it arrives.

Visualize:

Reflect:

June 21

You do not lose people since you do not own them. Relationships shift when people are being called elsewhere on the next phase of their sacred mission. There is no need to make judgments about this, it simply is how the rhythm of living in sacred calling works.

Visualize:

....

....

....

....

....

....

....

....

Reflect:

....

....

....

....

....

....

....

....

June 22

It is of high service to share your sacred gifts with others. It certainly blesses others, and you will notice that you will feel even more blessed that others feel when you do.

Visualize:

Reflect:

June 23

In divine perfection, there is acute awareness of infinite possibilities. When basking in limitless options, you become acutely aware of how infinite you are.

Visualize:

Reflect:

June 24

Life is meant to be experienced, not dreaded. If you are dreading life, that is a
clear sign that you have stepped out of divine perfection.

Visualize:

Reflect:

June 25

Asking for divine support each and every day is highly encouraged. Divine perfection wants to serve you, and it will to the degree that you ask.

Visualize:

....
....
....
....
....
....
....
....

Reflect:

....
....
....
....
....
....
....
....

June 26

Money is not the goal. Being fully resourced for your divine mission is.

Visualize:

Reflect:

June 27

Marriage is the distorted template. Sacred union is the divine truth. If you are feeling like things are misaligned in your partnership, your higher knowing is wanting out of the falsehood and into the golden arc of sacred union where there is divine truth and love that every person longs to return to.

Visualize:

Reflect:

June 28

Sometimes the greatest blessings come from the experiences that feel less than ideal. Be grateful for how they are fortifying you.

Visualize:

Reflect:

June 29

There is no need to seek answers when the heart leads.

Visualize:

Reflect:

June 30

You are always aligned. It is now a matter of looking at your life, seeing what you are actually aligning to, and then deciding if that is still something you choose.

Visualize:

....
....
....
....
....
....
....
....

Reflect:

....
....
....
....
....
....
....
....

JULY

Adventure

July 1

Soleil has codes of golden light waiting for you to claim.

Visualize:

Reflect:

July 2

The earth is eager for you to discover its beauty and miracles.

Visualize:

Reflect:

July 3

Don't let yourself be intimidated by the enormity of this world. Let yourself be truly and completely excited for it is nearly as limitless as you.

Visualize:

Reflect:

July 4

The future holds possibility, the present holds the full presence of you.

Visualize:

Reflect:

July 5

How wonderful that a new beginning is just a new adventure waiting to be taken.

Visualize:

....
....
....
....
....
....
....
....

Reflect:

....
....
....
....
....
....
....
....

July 6

The greatest adventure is remembering your sacred gifts so that you may share them with the world.

Visualize:

Reflect:

July 7

Imagine what you would see if you looked through the lens of divine perfection.

Visualize:

Reflect:

July 8

Exploring consciousness with awe and wonder is a blessing for your ascension.

Visualize:

Reflect:

July 9

Leading with love requires you to listen to your wise heart.

Visualize:

Reflect:

July 10

If you wish to become wiser, then you must experience more life, more people,
and more beauty.

Visualize:

Reflect:

July 11

Being in nature is the quickest way to step away from ego, and center into the rhythm of life, of you, of consciousness.

Visualize:

....
....
....
....
....
....
....
....

Reflect:

....
....
....
....
....
....
....
....

July 12

Desiring more enchantment in your life? Allow nature to remind you how to dance with it.

Visualize:

....

....

....

....

....

....

....

....

Reflect:

....

....

....

....

....

....

....

....

July 13

If you are bored, it's because you have decided to stop moving through life with curiosity.

Visualize:

....
....
....
....
....
....
....
....

Reflect:

....
....
....
....
....
....
....
....

July 14

Every person on earth is here because they are a contribution to the collective rhythm. Even if someone's journey does not make sense to you, it always makes sense to divine perfection.

Visualize:

Reflect:

July 15

The unknown is simply an unexplored adventure.

Visualize:

....
....
....
....
....
....
....
....

Reflect:

....
....
....
....
....
....
....

July 16

Pay attention to the vibrational nudges that excite you.

Visualize:

Reflect:

July 17

Choosing to be in full awareness eliminates the need to know everything now. Awareness is the divine compass that will make you aware of what you need to know now to move through the world with your sacred calling.

Visualize:

....
....
....
....
....
....
....
....

Reflect:

....
....
....
....
....
....
....
....

July 18

Bliss is already yours. You are simply remembering how to return to it and rest into it.

Visualize:

Reflect:

July 19

Analysis is simply misplaced wondering, that is, living in the wonder of you, the world, and consciousness. Stop wondering to answer questions and start wondering to see the bounty miracles and beauty already here for you to enjoy.

Visualize:

Reflect:

July 20

When the ego is served first, it disconnects you from the flow of blessings that are always present in divine perfection.

Visualize:

Reflect:

July 21

Many of your questions are acts of self abandonment. You already have awareness, questioning separates you from your highest knowing.

Visualize:

Reflect:

July 22

May you have the wisdom to know which journeys you're meant to take with others, and which ones you're meant to take alone.

Visualize:

Reflect:

July 23

We are all here to remember and restore the original codes.

Visualize:

....

....

....

....

....

....

....

....

Reflect:

....

....

....

....

....

....

....

....

July 24

Divine perfection desires to make your human experience exponentially easier.
When you choose it, you will discover this instantly.

Visualize:

Reflect:

July 25

Let everything go to see what stays.

Visualize:

Reflect:

July 26

Have fun playing with the magic of consciousness in motion.

Visualize:

....
....
....
....
....
....
....
....

Reflect:

....
....
....
....
....
....
....
....

July 27

Leave footprints of golden light wherever you go.

Visualize:

Reflect:

July 28

Be careful not to squander your days wishing for better ones.

Visualize:

Reflect:

July 29

Be the blessing to others that you often wished for in your past.

Visualize:

Reflect:

July 30

You can begin when you realize that this moment, now, is an adventure in and of itself.

Visualize:

Reflect:

July 31

Questioning what you once believed begins the process of liberation from your
mind, and initiates you into the codes inherent in divine perfection.

Visualize:

....
....
....
....
....
....
....
....

Reflect:

....
....
....
....
....
....
....
....

AUGUST

Connections

August 1

Gossiping and griping are misdirected ways to fulfill a deep human need: connection. Instead, discuss your vision, your passions, your grand ideas to enjoy the connection that you are actually desiring.

Visualize:

Reflect:

August 2

You are never too much or not enough. You are divine perfection.

Visualize:

Reflect:

August 3

Go where you are loved and appreciated. This is your golden standard.

Visualize:

....
....
....
....
....
....
....
....

Reflect:

....
....
....
....
....
....
....

August 4

People do not require saving, they require support in remembering their own potency.

Visualize:

Reflect:

August 5

When we realize how necessary we are to each other on this collective journey,
we stop judging and start appreciating.

Visualize:

Reflect:

August 6

If you are waiting to be ready before you take the next step on your sacred path,
you have decided to mistrust divine perfection

Visualize:

....
....
....
....
....
....
....
....

Reflect:

....
....
....
....
....
....
....
....

August 7

If someone costs you your inner peace, you cannot afford to have them in your life.

Visualize:

....
....
....
....
....
....
....
....

Reflect:

....
....
....
....
....
....
....
....

August 8

The best way to create emotional freedom is to practice neutrality and remember that nothing is personal, even if it feels like it is.

Visualize:

Reflect:

August 9

Reacting from your wounds and over responding from your truth will drastically change the quality of connection that you are seeking with others.

Visualize:

....
....
....
....
....
....
....
....

Reflect:

....
....
....
....
....
....
....
....

August 10

Be willing to hear what is not being said to enjoy being in full awareness. In full awareness you are equipped to make more aligned choices for your sacred path.

Visualize:

Reflect:

August 11

When you encounter people that don't feel aligned with your sacred path, keeping moving and shift your focus to being aware of the people who are aligned.

Visualize:

....
....
....
....
....
....
....
....

Reflect:

....
....
....
....
....
....
....
....

August 12

Awareness allows us to see the truth of all situations, versus the situations that are clouded by distortions or misplaced by hopes and expectations.

Visualize:

Reflect:

August 13

Relationships must be built on integrity. You cannot aim to please, but rather to connect. People pleasing undervalues your integrity with yourself.

Visualize:

Reflect:

August 14

You have no need to question anyone's intention when you choose to be aware of
their energy.

Visualize:

Reflect:

August 15

Harmony is the goal, versus balance. One is always present, the other is subjective.

Visualize:

....

....

....

....

....

....

....

....

Reflect:

....

....

....

....

....

....

....

....

August 16

Some of our greatest transformations of consciousness come when we are clear
on our sacred priorities.

Visualize:

Reflect:

August 17

Allow yourself to be excited about meeting the version of you that is truly free to *be.*

Visualize:

....
....
....
....
....
....
....
....

Reflect:

....
....
....
....
....
....
....

August 18

It requires far more energy to dim your light, versus being fully resourced to feel safe and supported in shining brightly.

Visualize:

Reflect:

August 19

If your energy dips, it is often a cue to pay attention to who you are surrounding yourself with.

Visualize:

Reflect:

August 20

You don't need approval, you desire belonging. You already belong, so there is no longer a need to seek.

Visualize:

Reflect:

August 21

There are people who want to celebrate the gift of you, simply because that is their nature. Be sure to call them into your world, so you can remember what divine connection feels like when it is grounded in this reality.

Visualize:

....
....
....
....
....
....
....
....

Reflect:

....
....
....
....
....
....
....
....

August 22

Your presence is a blessing to others. Your sacred gifts are the anointing to those willing to receive it.

Visualize:

Reflect:

August 23

Fully surrendering to divine perfection is the greatest opportunity in mastering
trust on your sacred path.

Visualize:

....
....
....
....
....
....
....

Reflect:

....
....
....
....
....
....
....

August 24

Harmonize your connections so that you are surrounded by contributors versus takers.

Visualize:

Reflect:

August 25

It is a gift to others when you allow yourself to receive the blessings that they
wish to bestow upon you.

Visualize:

....

....

....

....

....

....

....

....

Reflect:

....

....

....

....

....

....

....

....

August 26

Pure intentions can be felt without a single word.

Visualize:

Reflect:

August 27

There are many people who wish to support you simply because they desire to,
not because they want something in return.

Visualize:

....
....
....
....
....
....
....
....

Reflect:

....
....
....
....
....
....
....
....

August 28

There are no mysteries in divine perfection, there is only *being*.

Visualize:

Reflect:

August 29

Sacred stewardship will call you forward once you commit to your sacred mission.

Visualize:

....
....
....
....
....
....
....
....

Reflect:

....
....
....
....
....
....
....
....

August 30

The most powerful way to build connection is to *be*.

Visualize:

....

....

....

....

....

....

....

....

Reflect:

....

....

....

....

....

....

....

....

August 31

Focusing on what others are doing is a distraction from focusing on your own sacred path. It is time to allow others to *be*, so that you fully embrace your sacred calling.

Visualize:

Reflect:

SEPTEMBER

Wisdom

September 1

Ancient wisdom already resides within you. It reveals itself to you the more you are willing to remember it.

Visualize:

Reflect:

September 2

Every choice has a cause and effect. The greatest choice you can make for infinite miracles is choosing to live in divine perfection.

Visualize:

Reflect:

September 3

Answers do not exist outside of you. *You* are the answer, *you* hold the wisdom.

Visualize:

Reflect:

September 4

Trust, faith and surrender are all that are required in choosing a life aligned in divine perfection.

Visualize:

Reflect:

September 5

Shift from transforming and evolving, to remembering how to be moment to moment. The paradigm of perpetual healing journeys is not part of the new way.

Visualize:

Reflect:

September 6

Be an impeccable steward of your consciousness to enjoy greater access to your highest wisdom.

Visualize:

Reflect:

September 7

Release the need to figure things out. Delegate "the how" to divine perfection so that you are free to *be*.

Visualize:

....
....
....
....
....
....
....
....

Reflect:

....
....
....
....
....
....
....
....

September 8

There are different routes to the same destination. The most aligned route is that of divine perfection.

Visualize:

Reflect:

September 9

In divine perfection, nothing is personal. People's responses to you are simply information that allows you to be aware of what *is* aligned for you, and what *isn't*. Wisdom allows you to hold neutrality.

Visualize:

....

....

....

....

....

....

....

....

Reflect:

....

....

....

....

....

....

....

....

September 10

You are already divine perfection. Allow it to be your guide and your wisdom keeper.

Visualize:

Reflect:

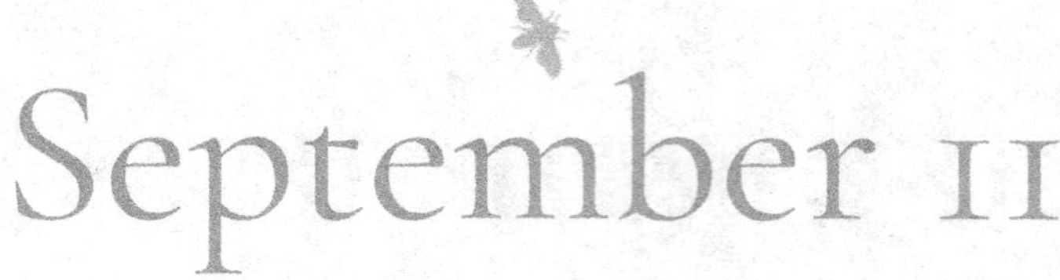

September 11

You are here by divine design, and your sacred wisdom is needed by others.

Visualize:

Reflect:

September 12

Your sacred path must be walked to gather the wisdom required to bless you and others.

Visualize:

Reflect:

September 13

Others have wisdom for you to receive for your sacred path. Living in isolation
deprives you of the necessary wisdom to support your divine calling.

Visualize:

....
....
....
....
....
....
....
....

Reflect:

....
....
....
....
....
....
....
....

September 14

Everything you need is already within you, or is on its way to you.

Visualize:

Reflect:

September 15

You always have access to an infinite supply of resources. They are not seen my the mind but are clear and present in divine perfection.r on its way to you.

Visualize:

....
....
....
....
....
....
....
....

Reflect:

....
....
....
....
....
....
....
....

September 16

Your golden light requires to lead others out of the abyss of distortions so that they may see their sacred path clearly.

Visualize:

Reflect:

September 17

Being busy is your cue to pay attention to the wisdom of your body and your sacred calling desiring movement.

Visualize:

Reflect:

September 18

Earth is a finite trip for your sacred path, the divine heart beat is where home is.

Visualize:

Reflect:

September 19

Your past cannot change, but you can allow it to inform your wisdom so that you may bless others with it.

Visualize:

Reflect:

September 20

You are allowed to change your perspective when new wisdom appears that feels more aligned than what you knew before.

Visualize:

Reflect:

September 21

Achieving enlightenment isn't the goal. You already are light, and now the calling is to create lightness in all aspects of your being for greater awareness to appear.

Visualize:

....

....

....

....

....

....

....

....

Reflect:

....

....

....

....

....

....

....

September 22

Being nice and being kind are two different energies. One can be created through acting while the other is spread through character.

Visualize:

Reflect:

September 23

You have all the time that you need. Time expands for you in divine perfection.

Visualize:

Reflect:

September 24

Seeking an obstructed path is a sign that you are attempting to follow someone else's. When a path is meant for you to take, it will become crystal clear and will flow in your favor.

Visualize:

Reflect:

September 25

Thinking is your attempt to reach higher states of wisdom. It's simply not the most aligned portal to get there.

Visualize:

Reflect:

September 26

You can seek the Divine in the outside world, but the real discovery begins when you realize it already resides within you.

Visualize:

Reflect:

September 27

Positivity is forced, joy is the natural state that you are actually desiring.

Visualize:

Reflect:

September 28

The focus isn't on eliminating darkness, it is in discovering the beauty on the earth plane. The beauty will illuminate so that the darkness fades away.

Visualize:

Reflect:

September 29

Your wisdom is the teacher and the blessing for you and others.

Visualize:

Reflect:

September 30

Your wisdom already knows. Allow it to show you the clear direction you are seeking.

Visualize:

Reflect:

OCTOBER

Manifesting

October 1

Motivation is no longer relevant when honoring your sacred calling. It is so inspiring that it blesses you with the vitality required to hold it at a high frequency.

Visualize:

....

....

....

....

....

....

....

....

Reflect:

....

....

....

....

....

....

....

October 2

You can plant and harvest seeds of creation any time of year.

Visualize:

Reflect:

October 3

Divine perfection is the quickest most aligned space to manifest.

Visualize:

Reflect:

October 4

When you call forward your desires, you are allowed to ask for more if you have
already outgrown your initial request.

Visualize:

Reflect:

October 5

Thinking your way into your desires is creating from ego, feeling into what creates instant joy will bring you even greater delights.

Visualize:

....
....
....
....
....
....
....
....

Reflect:

....
....
....
....
....
....
....

October 6

The golden key to manifesting anything is stepping into divine perfection before making your request.

Visualize:

Reflect:

October 7

Ask often. You are allowed to receive all that you desire. You are allowed to have second helpings.

Visualize:

Reflect:

October 8

Liquid gold is already overflowing in your money pots. You do not need to see it to claim it.

Visualize:

....

....

....

....

....

....

....

....

Reflect:

....

....

....

....

....

....

....

....

October 9

Control creates struggle, not miracles.

Visualize:

Reflect:

October 10

You are a wise being who radiates light. Have faith in your ability to manifest wonderful things in your life.

Visualize:

Reflect:

October 11

You are already worthy of receiving.

Visualize:

Reflect:

October 12

Expand your capacity to receive by visualizing a larger container to hold all that you desire.

Visualize:

Reflect:

October 13

You are allowed to thrive when others around you are not. Fairness is a
distortion, it is subjective and not of divine perfection.

Visualize:

....
....
....
....
....
....
....
....

Reflect:

....
....
....
....
....
....
....
....

October 14

It is wonderful to dream, it is even more delightful to ask for those dreams to come to life with the loving support of divine perfection.

Visualize:

....
....
....
....
....
....
....
....

Reflect:

....
....
....
....
....
....
....

October 15

When you are fully aligned to and walking your sacred path, what you desire is different, what is required to bring into form is different. The sacred path requires full resourcing so asking regularly is a requirement.

Visualize:

Reflect:

October 16

Receiving is about you allowing creation to bless you for all that you *be*.

Visualize:

Reflect:

October 17

The Field of Imagination holds infinite creativity for dreaming even bigger than you imagined was possible.

Visualize:

Reflect:

October 18

Allow your desires to be louder than your doubts.

Visualize:

Reflect:

October 19

The Field of Infinite Possibilities teaches you that there are a myriad of ways to
bring your desires into form.

Visualize:

....
....
....
....
....
....
....
....

Reflect:

....
....
....
....
....
....
....

October 20

You are already capable of handling the desires that are on their way to you.

Visualize:

Reflect:

October 21

Manifesting your plan is very different from surrendering to the manifestations
of the divine plan.

Visualize:

....
....
....
....
....
....
....
....

Reflect:

....
....
....
....
....
....
....
....

October 22

Speak to your womb of creation every day to explore what hidden desires are
ready to be revealed and received.

Visualize:

Reflect:

October 23

Worry is a wet blanket to manifesting more wealth.

Visualize:

....
....
....
....
....
....
....
....

Reflect:

....
....
....
....
....
....
....
....

October 24

You have the sacred power of speaking your dreams into existence in a nano second.

Visualize:

Reflect:

October 25

Receiving your manifestations with gratitude brings even more blessings your way.

Visualize:

....
....
....
....
....
....
....
....

Reflect:

....
....
....
....
....
....
....
....

October 26

Allow infinite creation to surprise and delight beyond what you ever knew was possible.

Visualize:

Reflect:

October 27

You are already manifesting in every moment. This is why being an impeccable steward of your consciousness is essential in manifesting what you truly desire.

Visualize:

....

....

....

....

....

....

....

....

Reflect:

....

....

....

....

....

....

....

....

October 28

Bring your sacred heart into all that you desire so that your manifestations are always calibrated to that frequency.

Visualize:

Reflect:

October 29

You are allowed to have more than you need. You are not greedy, you are a first class receiver.

Visualize:

....

....

....

....

....

....

....

....

Reflect:

....

....

....

....

....

....

....

....

October 30

Manifesting money with ease starts with seeing it as a tool for creation.

Visualize:

Reflect:

October 31

Money wants to be on your dream team and bring your dreams to life. Allow it
to have a seat at the table and contribute to your sacred vision.

Visualize:

....
....
....
....
....
....
....
....

Reflect:

....
....
....
....
....
....
....
....

NOVEMBER

Gratitude

November 1

Gratitude is automatic when choosing to live in divine perfection.

Visualize:

Reflect:

November 2

There is always a reason to be grateful when we choose to look for it.

Visualize:

Reflect:

November 3

Accept all that you manifest as a gift. In this manner you will always be grateful.

Visualize:

....
....
....
....
....
....
....
....

Reflect:

....
....
....
....
....
....
....
....

November 4

Be grateful to the version of you that brought you here.

Visualize:

Reflect:

November 5

Overwhelm is easily remedied with gratitude gives.

Visualize:

....
....
....
....
....
....
....
....

Reflect:

....
....
....
....
....
....
....
....

November 6

Be grateful for how your bed holds you in moments of rest.

Visualize:

Reflect:

November 7

Adopt a new attitude: the attitude of gratitude!

Visualize:

Reflect:

November 8

Give thanks as if you already have all that you desire.

Visualize:

Reflect:

November 9

Don't get so bogged down in the obstacles that you miss the gift that is today.

Visualize:

Reflect:

November 10

Be grateful for the amenities in your space that provide comfort.

Visualize:

Reflect:

November 11

Gratitude is one of the greatest magnets for manifesting your heart's desires.

Visualize:

Reflect:

November 12

Be grateful for the divine codes that you receive from the sun. It is not blinding you, it is showering you with rays of golden light that give you energy and deep connection to heaven on earth.

Visualize:

Reflect:

November 13

Surrender yourself to gratitude. Say it. Write it. Love it. Don't just do those things. You must also be in gratitude, from moment to moment.

Visualize:

....
....
....
....
....
....
....
....

Reflect:

....
....
....
....
....
....
....
....

November 14

Be grateful for your inner guidance as it serves you in walking with ease on your sacred path.

Visualize:

Reflect:

November 15

Be grateful for the animals that share their sacred medicine in support of your divine mission.

Visualize:

....
....
....
....
....
....
....
....

Reflect:

....
....
....
....
....
....
....
....

November 16

Be grateful for the version of your spirit that chose to be on earth at this time.

Visualize:

Reflect:

November 17

Be grateful for the people that you have met along the way, especially the people that contributed to you fully stepping into your sacred calling.

Visualize:

Reflect:

November 18

Always thank yourself for asking for something you need or desire.

Visualize:

Reflect:

November 19

Thank those who walk out of your life equally as you thank those who walk into
it.

Visualize:

....
....
....
....
....
....
....
....

Reflect:

....
....
....
....
....
....
....
....

November 20

Gratitude is a sacred elixir for your heart.

Visualize:

Reflect:

November 21

If you are grateful for new opportunities that are on their way to you, even if they are invisible at the moment, then you will easily receive them.

Visualize:

Reflect:

November 22

Be grateful for this day of untapped possibility.

Visualize:

Reflect:

November 23

Gratitude is a principle to live life by.

Visualize:

Reflect:

November 24

Gratitude is one of the greatest magnets for manifesting your heart's desires.

Visualize:

Reflect:

November 25

Grateful people are easy and joyful to be around. If you are wishing to connect with more people, a grateful state will easily call more people in to enjoy life with.

Visualize:

Reflect:

November 26

Watch how your life changes when you start thanking the divine instead of questioning it.

Visualize:

Reflect:

November 27

Be grateful for your wisdom.

Visualize:

Reflect:

November 28

Gratitude truly is the gift that keeps on giving.

Visualize:

Reflect:

November 29

Aim to be the person who brings joy into every space they enter.

Visualize:

Reflect:

November 30

Gratitude is one of the quickest boosts to personal frequency. Feeling low? Find something to be grateful for now.

Visualize:

....
....
....
....
....
....
....
....

Reflect:

....
....
....
....
....
....
....
....

DECEMBER
Celebration

December 1

You are divine. And just like the Divine, you are to be honored and revered.

Visualize:

....
....
....
....
....
....
....

Reflect:

....
....
....
....
....
....
....

December 2

Your inner self knows that the small victories aren't so small.

Visualize:

Reflect:

December 3

No matter what has happened today, you have cause to celebrate something.

Visualize:

....
....
....
....
....
....
....
....

Reflect:

....
....
....
....
....
....
....
....

December 4

When you celebrate your greatness, you are celebrating yourself as the miracle.

Visualize:

Reflect:

December 5

Celebrate the version of you that did not give up, even when that seemed like the only option.

Visualize:

....
....
....
....
....
....
....
....

Reflect:

....
....
....
....
....
....
....
....

December 6

When you receive a crown load of a download, it's time to celebrate!

Visualize:

Reflect:

December 7

Celebrate your willingness to grow, even when it is uncomfortable.

Visualize:

....

....

....

....

....

....

....

....

Reflect:

....

....

....

....

....

....

....

....

December 8

Celebrate the version of you that was willing to walk your sacred path even
when the majority of your path has been a mystery to your mind.

Visualize:

Reflect:

December 9

Your body requires celebration, not judgment.

Visualize:

Reflect:

December 10

Celebrate the version of you that is no longer triggered by people that used to get under your skin.

Visualize:

Reflect:

December 11

Honor yourself today as the brave being that chose to be on earth at this time.

Visualize:

Reflect:

December 12

The best way to live is as perpetual celebration versus a project that needs to be improved.

Visualize:

Reflect:

December 13

Little miracles are just as worthy of celebration of the big miracles, starting with this "now" moment.

Visualize:

Reflect:

December 14

Live your life in celebration of your existence.

Visualize:

Reflect:

December 15

You are a magnet for miracles and that is cause for celebration!

Visualize:

Reflect:

December 16

Celebrate the joys of others as frequently as your own.

Visualize:

Reflect:

December 17

Divine perfection celebrates you in all of your humanness and can teach you how to do the same.

Visualize:

Reflect:

December 18

If you want joy, *be* joy

Visualize:

Reflect:

December 19

Celebrate each new awareness of the magic of you.

Visualize:

....

....

....

....

....

....

....

....

Reflect:

....

....

....

....

....

....

....

....

December 20

It is your divine birthright to enjoy abundance on all levels.

Visualize:

Reflect:

December 21

When you love life, it shows you that love has always been there for you.

Visualize:

Reflect:

December 22

Make a list of activities that bring you instant joy and treat them as daily priorities.

Visualize:

Reflect:

December 23

Your kindness is contagious. Be the golden thread of kindness for others and
spread it far and wide.

Visualize:

Reflect:

December 24

Take a breath. It is *all* connected.

Visualize:

Reflect:

December 25

Go where you are celebrated for the gift of you.

Visualize:

Reflect:

December 26

Celebrate others the way you would like to be celebrated.

Visualize:

Reflect:

December 27

Create a celebration ritual to devote yourself to.

Visualize:

....
....
....
....
....
....
....
....

Reflect:

....
....
....
....
....
....
....
....

December 28

What a gift this day is.

Visualize:

Reflect:

December 29

You belong, you matter, your life has meaning beyond words. That is the celebration.

Visualize:

Reflect:

December 30

Each time you celebrate, love, or honor yourself and others, you raise the
vibration of the collective.

Visualize:

Reflect:

December 31

Sometimes you might ask, "how can I believe in miracles when this situation is happening in my life?" The real question is how can you not expect them in a universe full of infinite possibilities?

Visualize:

Reflect:

About the Author

Jennifer is an award winning CEO, 11 time best selling author and founder of the #1 Akashic Record Training School in the world. Over the past eleven years, her school has certified over 100,000 consultants in over 100 countries and has been translated into five languages.

She is also a clear channel for Mother Malia, The Great Mother, who comes to earth during times of great transition, like the collective ascension we are experiencing now. She is here to restore the original codes of The Land of The People, to reawaken the gold codes as they were intended and support as many light leaders as possible elevate into their sacred mission and allow in millions to fuel the spread of their sacred gifts.

When she is not channeling and providing high level strategic guidance to light leaders, you can find her enjoying trips with her family, hikes with her dog, or tending to her rare plant collection.